The Broken Candle

Written by Helen Sebastian
Ilustrated/Design Layout by Jan Asleson

Copyright © 2017 Helen Sebastian

All rights reserved. No part of this book may be reproduced in any form or by any electronic or mechanical means, including information storage and retrieval systems, without permission in writing from the publisher, except by reviewers, who may quote brief passages in a review.

ISBN 9780692991930

Library of Congress Control Number 20194053

Printed in the United States of America by Ingram Spark/Lightning Source

Published by Spirit Wings Designs 2017
daslpacker55@yahoo.com
Visit at www.spiritwingsdesigns.com

hswilson1935@hotmail.com

The Broken Candle

by

Helen Sebastian

Illustrations by Jan Asleson

"Let your light shine before men, that they may see your good works, and glorify your Father, who is in heaven."

 Matthew 5:16

This story begins when Travis was given the "bag" on Sunday evening, September 15, 1996.

Following the Sunday evening song service, boys and girls would be called down to the front of the Sanctuary and gather around Pastor Jim for his object lesson from the "bag". It was a special privilege to be given the bag, find unusual items, then bring it back for the next Sunday. Boys and girls would think it fun to try to find unusual objects to place in the bag, then see how Pastor Jim would be able to tell a story around that object.

Travis was so excited when he was handed the bag to bring back the following Sunday.

Before he got home that evening, he already knew what he wanted to take, a candle.

He wanted a good candle, one that was not scarred or broken. Grandma helped him look for this very special candle. When one was found they carefully wrapped it in tissue paper and placed it into the bag.

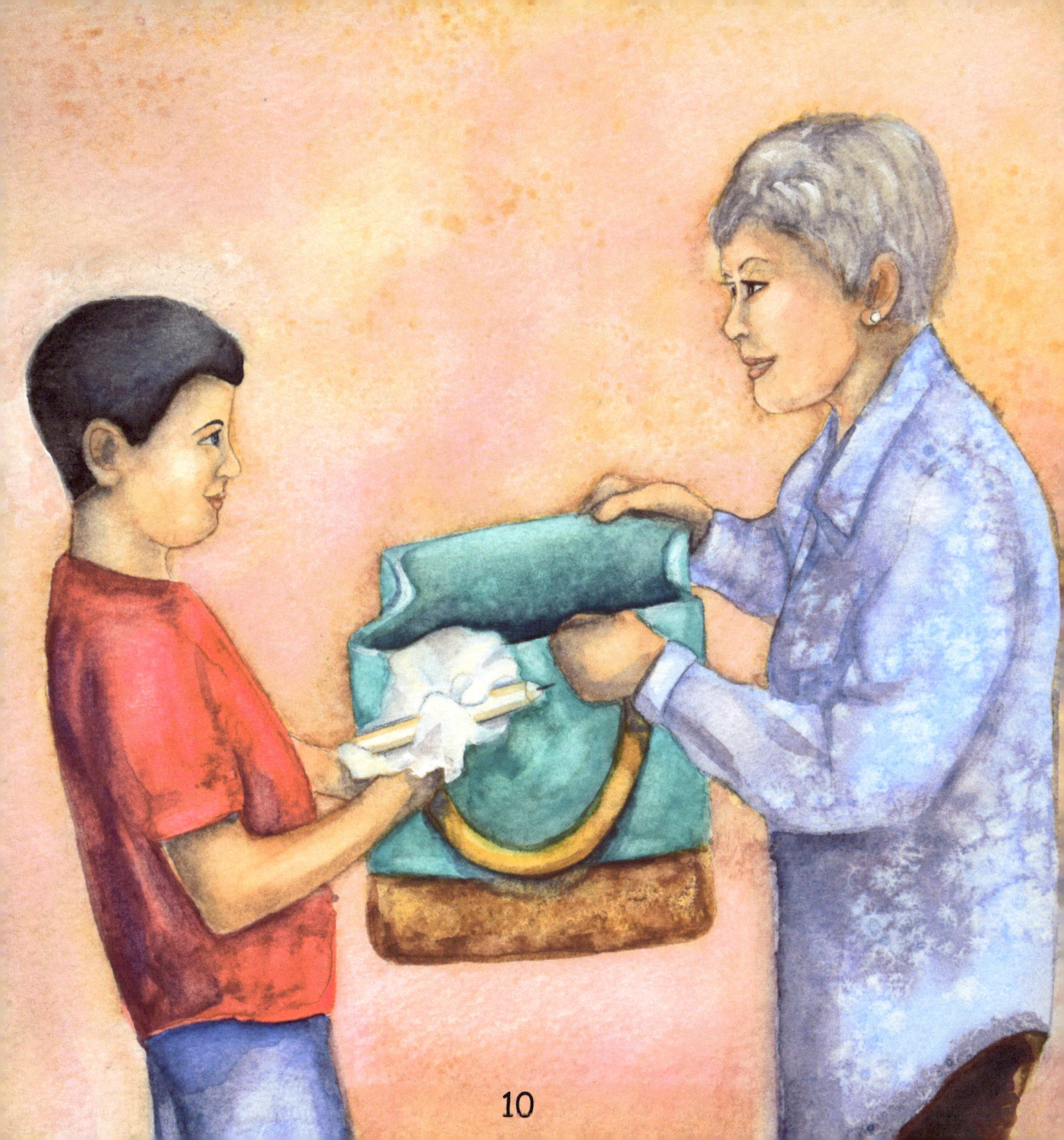

The following Sunday evening Grandma had a scheduled meeting in the church library, so he came early with her. While he waited for church to begin, he sat outside on the church step and watched his brother, Matthew, play ball across the street with the youth during JAM (Jesus and Me).

As he was watching, he stood up and accidentally dropped the candle. "Oh, dear, I hope my candle is not broken!" As he took it out of the bag, it didn't feel quite right.

He carefully unwrapped the tissue paper and saw in horror that the candle was broken into two pieces and was only held together by the wick.

Heartbroken, he rushed inside to show the broken candle to his Grandmother and said, "I cannot take this candle. It's ugly and broken!" "Oh yes you can", replied Grandma. "I know Pastor Jim will use the candle to tell a good story."

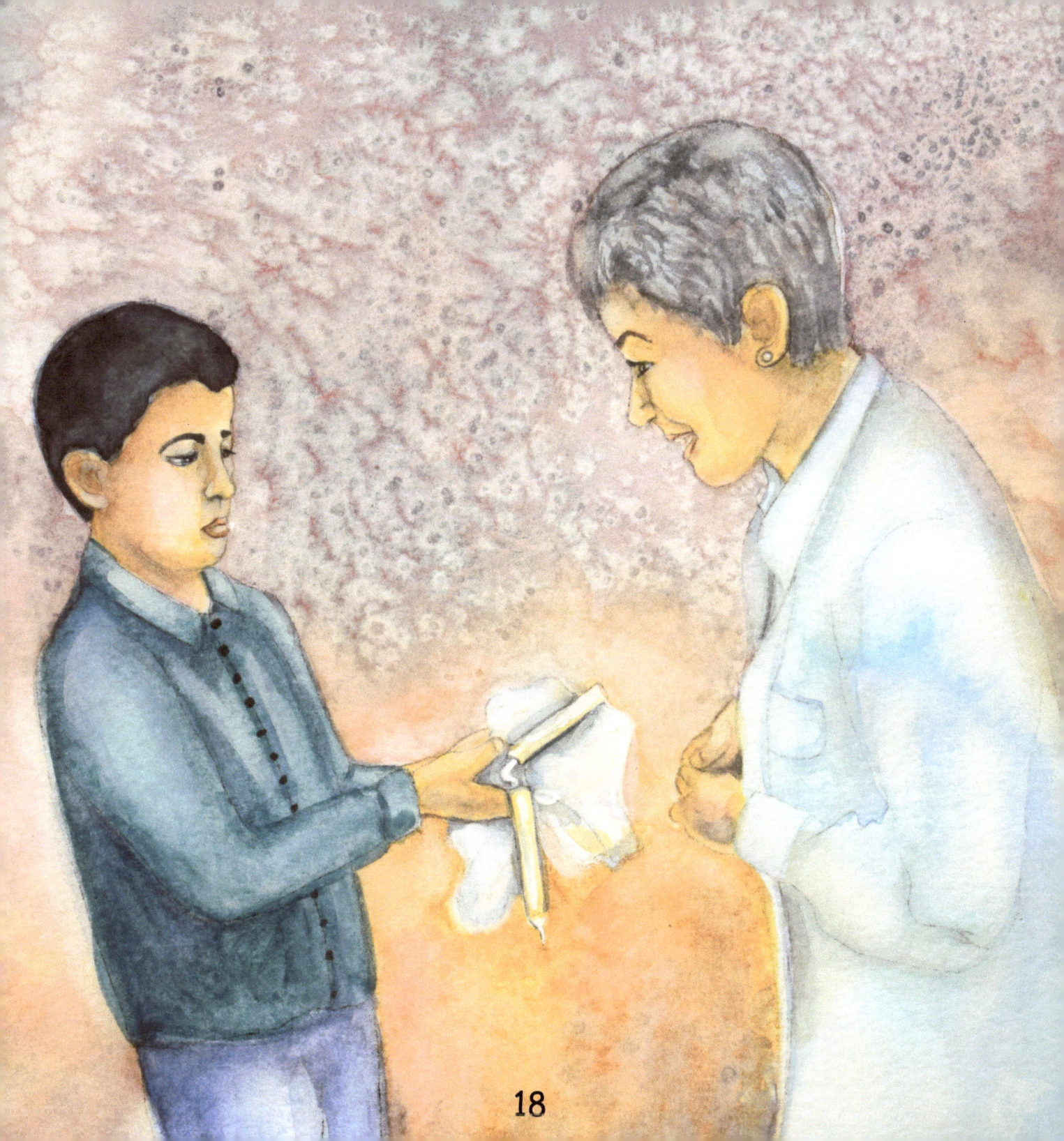

When it came time for the boys and girls to come down for their story, Travis nervously picked up the bag containing the broken candle and carried it down to the front. He felt scared because of what the other boys and girls and Pastor Jim might think or say. When Pastor Jim asked who had brought the bag, Travis slowly handed it to him. He was afraid to look at Pastor fearing what he might say.

When the candle was taken

out of the bag, there was

a discussion about the

candle being ugly and broken.

"Oh, why didn't I just throw

the bag and candle away,"

thought Travis.

Pastor Jim carefully looked at the broken candle, back to Travis, then at the children gathered around him and said, "Boys and girls, sometimes we are broken physically and emotionally, even though we are Christians."

He then held up the two broken pieces that were held together by one long wick and continued. "This wick, which runs the entire length of the candle represents the Holy Spirit which dwells within us."

He then lit the candle and had someone turn off the lights in the Sanctuary. "Even though the candle is broken", he said, "it still continues to give off light." A pretty light was held up so the members could see. The dark Sanctuary became lighter as the candle glowed brightly. Then he said to the children, "No matter how broken we are as Christians, we will always have the indwelling Holy Spirit and no person can ever take His Presence from us."

"I'm so happy that I didn't throw this candle away", thought Travis to himself. "God can use good from something that is broken."

Helen Sebastian
Author/Publisher

Helen graduated from Caney High School in Caney, Kansas in 1953. She then graduated with an Associate of Arts degree from the following colleges: Coffeyville Junior College, in Coffeyville, Kansas, Pittsburg State College with a B.S. in Education, and the University of Kansas with an M.S. in Education.

In 1994 she retired after teaching for thirty-six years in the third and fourth grades. Following retirement she volunteered to work in the St. Andrew's school library for 18-years. During this period she also tutored many children after school and during the summer. She did not accept any pay for tutoring because to her, helping children and watching them achieve was the purpose.

Helen taught the fourth and fifth grade Sunday School class in the First Baptist Church for around fifteen years.
At the present time she is a co-teacher in the fourth and fifth grade Sunday School.

Jan Asleson
Illustrator

My designs are inspired by a desire to share with others the beauty that I see around me. My passion is to encourage others through my artistic mediums to not give up on their dreams, to recognize the Blessings all around them and to know that there is always hope. In my life journey to know who I am, I've discovered that what I've come to recognize as true art comes for the greatest Artist of all, God. I believe that when we connect with each other on a heart to heart level, our lives can be changed for the good. I hope that in some way my art will touch your heart...

I find my creativity in the mediums of oil, acrylic, pastels, watercolor, metals, leather, silk art and natural textiles. I also create works of art in commissioned portraits, greeting cards, prints and fine jewelry designs and creations. I live in South-East Kansas with my husband David.

You can find me at www.spiritwingsdesigns.com

This Little Light of Mine

This little light of mine, I'm gonna let it shine.
This little light of mine, I'm gonna let it shine.
This little light of mine, I'm gonna let it shine.
Let it shine, Let it shine, Let it shine!

Shine all over the world, I'm gonna let it shine.
Shine all over the world, I'm gonna let it shine.
Shine all over the world, I'm gonna let it shine.
Let it shine, Let it shine, Let it shine!

Everywhere I go, I'm gonna let it shine.
Everywhere I go, I'm gonna let it shine.
Everywhere I go, I'm gonna let it shine.
Let it shine, Let it shine, Let it shine!

Under a bushel Oh no!, I'm gonna let it shine.
Under a bushel Oh no!, I'm gonna let it shine.
Under a bushel Oh no!, I'm gonna let it shine.
Let it shine, All the time, Let it shine.

Jesus gave it to me, I'm gonna let it shine.
Jesus gave it to me, I'm gonna let it shine.
Jesus gave it to me, I'm gonna let it shine.
Let it shine, Let it shine, Let it shine!

Lyrics: Written by Harry Dixon Loes, 1895-1965

www.ingramcontent.com/pod-product-compliance
Lightning Source LLC
Chambersburg PA
CBHW042147290426
44110CB00003B/142